ATOMS AND MOLECULES OF AN ALCHEMIST

Twenty-Nine Love Poems
and an Epilogue

Omar Rodríguez

ISBN-13: 9798501657717

Cover by Remedios Varo: Fenómeno de Ingravidez, 1963. By license from Artists Rights Society. © 2021 Remedios Varo, Artists Rights Society (ARS), New York / VEGAP, Madrid. Procedencia de la imagen, Banco de Imágenes VEGAP. Image from VEGAP Images Bank.

Library of Congress Control Number: 2021909933
Printed in the United States of America

CONTENTS

Title Page

Copyright

Foreword   1

Acknowledgements   3

Introduction   5

Atoms and Molecules of an Alchemist   7

1 Metaphysical Theorem   9

2 Chess Piece   13

3 Refuge for Me, Your Body   15

4 The Indiscreet Pupils of My Eyes   17

5 Certainty of You   19

6 In Need of You   21

7 Tonight   25

8 Strange Phenomenon   27

9 I Lend You My Freedom   29

10 Prisoner Without a Prison   33

11 The Talisman   35

12 Metaphysical Discovery 39

13 I and You 41

14 Clinging to You 45

15 Key-Losing Friend 49

16 The Memories Weaver 55

17 The Alchemist's Imprisonment 59

18 The Ultimatum 65

19 The Abortion 69

20 I Hang My Handkerchief to Dry 75

21 The Shipwreck 77

22 Ashes 79

23 Metaphysical Jigsaw Puzzle 81

24 That's It! 87

25 Freeing the Prisoner 93

26 Beyond You 95

27 The Closed Store 99

28 What Does It Matter! 101

29 Fourteen Metaphysical Reflections 105

Epilogue: Conversations with My Past Self 111

The Author 117

FOREWORD

Omar's poems take us on a journey through his past, and anyone who has ever fallen in or out of love will recognize the landscape. His poems are intensely personal and passionate, sensual and seductive. With the courage of an explorer, the eye of a master jeweler, and the patience of an archaeologist, he investigates and examines the nuances of love, lust, loss and longing.

His work is imbued with an almost clinical clarity. He writes about what the mind needs and what the heart desires. In short, he's interested in what we humans need and want from each other, not just to survive but to flourish.

Like a detective sifting for clues, he'll unearth memories and stir up long forgotten feelings - of sadness, of regret, even pain...such as the pain from the sting of a lover's rejection or the humiliation of a lover's indifference. But he'll also find moments of joy and delight, like the gift of an unexpected smile, the comfort of a reassuring touch, or the sigh that speaks volumes about the things left unsaid.

Omar doesn't indulge in emotional reveries or bask in the warm glow of familiar feelings. He is driven by the realization that the past is always present and that a fierce reckoning is needed to achieve, if not a reconciliation, at least a truce between the man he was then and the man he might yet become.

These poems are an invitation to join him on a quest. All you'll need to take the journey is an open mind, a restless curiosity and a beating heart. It will be a journey that is both illuminating and intoxicating and a journey well worth the taking.

John Montague

ACKNOWLEDGE-MENTS

I thank my friends who read parts of the draft of my English translation, gave me feedback or technical advice and were so supportive in publishing this English edition: John Montague, Glen Goodman, Mindy Lewis, Munawar Noorani and Margreet Van de Griend.

OMAR RODRÍGUEZ

INTRODUCTION

This is not a conventional poetry book.

It describes the first steps of my personal journey in search for meaning and a romantic partner. I felt then as lost as the mythical alchemist, in search for the impossible. I was in the metaphysical and confusing world of emotions, bound by the realities of daily life and yet under the influence of cosmic science.

The epilogue was written many years later.

My feelings are often described using scientific terms uncommon in poetry like molecules, atoms, microscopes, light beams, Verniers and Geiger counters. And sometimes I use mundane artifacts like the telephone, a dresser in a room and effervescent tablets bought in the drugstore. I suppose I was trying to build a bridge in my logical mind between what was real and touchable and what was ethereal and metaphysical. I was trying to make logical sense of the illogical.

Although those who inspired most of these poems are now a distant memory for me, the feelings and emotions they triggered are still very fresh. I learned a lot about myself through my interactions with them. They contributed fully to my life.

This is a record of my early journey.

I hope it echoes yours.

And if you are right now in such a journey, enjoy every minute of it and pay attention. And rest assured that time heals everything.

You can find the Spanish version of this book in Amazon.com as *Átomos y Moléculas de un Alquimista.*

ATOMS AND MOLECULES OF AN ALCHEMIST

OMAR RODRÍGUEZ

1 METAPHYSICAL THEOREM

*Correcting the Math
Professor's Certainty*

The old math professor
and geometry expert postulates
with singular certainty
and with no scientific doubt whatsoever
a theorem well known by us all
which states that
a straight line is the shortest distance between two points.

But this learned silver haired professor is mistaken.

He is mistaken. I am certain he is mistaken.

I know with firm certainty
that the shortest distance

is no straight line, no
but a passionate kiss
from your lips.

A kiss that
ties me up
imprisons me
binds me
overwhelms me
confuses my taste while I savor it
pulls me in
distracts me
triggers in me a palpitating sigh
stuns me
makes me dizzy
and accelerates my pulse with the rare power
almost alchemical
to make me fly, helplessly to the clouds.

Yes, it is a fact.
The professor is mistaken this time around.
His methods are unsound

his theorem imprecise
although he does have an excuse:
he has never tasted your lips.

I myself found out one day
quite by accident.
The sensitive nerves of my lips and my
tongue told me
and my skin sensed it
transforming themselves into an extension
of you.
Unlimited, unbound, with no molecular
gaps.

By an alchemical miracle and for an instant
we got transformed into one body
fused, alert and expectant.

From that day on
I became attached to you
molecularly fused with you
strongly tied by the invisible

yet metaphysically inscrutable pull
of your lips and your mouth
that got me closer to you by a distance
infinitely shorter
than the distance imprecisely postulated
by the old learned professor and geometry
expert.

But don't you worry
dear old math professor.
I won't reveal to anyone
that your theorem is mistaken.

I will never confront your science.
I will keep your secret in silence
with the kaleidoscopic but hopeful certainty
that I will one day kiss those lips again.

And in the meantime, I will scientifically
record this discovery
in the passionate scribblings
of this silly note book.

2 CHESS PIECE

The Mysterious Metaphysical Chessboard

I am a chess piece
playing, unknowingly
different and changing roles.

Bishop, castle, knight and queen
and sometimes modest pawn
whose movement
serves to protect
unbeknownst to me
pieces more important
and to save
sometimes with my own life
prismatic and kaleidoscopic moves
designed by the superior
and incomprehensible logic
of a chess master.

OMAR RODRÍGUEZ

3 REFUGE FOR ME, YOUR BODY

The Alchemist's Prayer

efuge for me
your body.

Refuge for you
my arms.

Tremor in my voice
your breathing.

Tremor in your back
my touch.

Warmth in my skin
your torso.

Extension of your hand
my body.

Sanctuary for me
your shoulder
where the atoms of my soul
safely sleep.

Atoms that I open freely to you now
as I feel shelter in your eyes
and warmth in your words
and the taste of your lips
and the velvet sound of
your voice.

4 THE INDISCREET PUPILS OF MY EYES

*Experiencing
Metaphysical Nakedness*

Do you want to know me in an instant?

Watch me carefully
scan my eyes
let yourself be guided by the indiscreet
pupils of my eyes.

I could be nude, stripped naked before you
without the slightest sign of shame
but I would blush immediately
under your careful gaze
scanning the dilating pupils of my eyes
beyond the blinking lashes.

They will tell you in an instant
what you don't know about me
…and even that about me
which I don't know myself.

5 CERTAINTY OF YOU

*Getting Ready for a Future
and Certain Encounter*

One day I will find you
because I am sure you exist
even if, so far
I don't know your name or your face
or have felt the warmth of your body
yet.

I know that I will find you
in some random twist of my path
waiting for me
as lonely as me
longing for me even if
you don't know my name or my face
or have felt the warmth of my body
either.

I am certain that every step

every failed attempt
every disappointment
every disillusion
every ridicule
and every new experience
will take me closer to you.

They are teaching me to be ready
with open antennas
and tuned in receptors
for that magical and unknown day
when we will find each other
to finally share our life together.

6 IN NEED OF YOU

The Awakening of the Alchemist

This Sunday morning
as I woke up
alone
in my bedroom
I wished you were next to me.

When I opened my eyes
and saw your absence
and felt my missing you
I hugged my pillow
closed my eyes, and fantasized about you.

And for an instant
of magical completeness

I overcame the frustration of your absence
imagining:
- the warm feel of your legs and your torso
- the delicious sweet bitterness of your lips
and your mouth
- the playful and unpredictable touch of your
hands
which all felt so familiar, although mostly
unknown to me.

And for that brief instant I filled myself with
you.

When I opened my eyes again
and saw myself in my bedroom, alone and
with empty hands
I became aware, for the first time
of this new
awakening
playful and at the same time worrisome

need of you.

And after a long and pleasant sigh
I closed my eyes again
to keep dreaming.

OMAR RODRÍGUEZ

7 TONIGHT

Looking for You

I will dress myself tonight
in my hidden-terror uniform:

- colorful shirt
- casual tight-fitted jeans
- fashionable shoes
- my face wearing ultra-bright smile #2
- and my soul broken and in pieces
assembled together with adhesive tape
recently bought at the stationery store.

Those fragile and prismatic pieces
are so close to end up molecularly split –yet
again--
at the end of this night.
And maybe this time forever.

Curious dancing little crystals they are
breaking apart every night more and more...

Maybe one day
I shall put them together
to reveal your image
in the stained-glass window of a church.

And maybe then
I will know your name
and see your face
and touch your body
at last.

8 STRANGE PHENOMENON

*Surrendering the
Control Panel*

Your breath, in my lips.
Your voice, in my ear.
Your pulse, in my chest.
Your scent, in my nose.
And your firm masculine touch, on the hot
dermis of my skin.

Metaphysical osmosis
formed by electric
invisible and sensitive fluids
lit by iridescent and colorful sparkles
which speed up the cardiac muscle
and trigger chain reactions
of difficult control and high risk.

OMAR RODRÍGUEZ

You and I sunk in a tiny area
in the bright beam of a microscope
without any sense of space or time.

You and I, in a different dimension
of cosmic walls
and worrisome consequences
that I refuse this time
to scan through the analytic filter
of my control panel.

9 I LEND YOU MY FREEDOM

Proposing Parameters and Game Rules

I lend you my freedom
so that you shelter it.

I share with you my loneliness
so that you fill it.

I present you my soul
so that you make it whole.

I offer you my body
so that you touch it.

The timeframe will be as long as the rest of
my life

or as short as an instant
and it will be as long as our wills
want to share their selves with each other
without losing their own individuality.

But love, don't ever ask me
to gift them all to you.

Time, soul, loneliness and body
I only have one of each.

If I gift them to you now
what would I have
to give to you later?

I do not, and never will belong to anyone, my
love
but to my own self.

I open my heart to you

in exchange for you opening yours to me.

Let's walk in this path together
as long as our own loneliness wants to
or is able to
without losing our selves
which is what most attracts me to you:
your self.

And God willing
that from our shared loneliness
we are able together to give birth to companionship
good memories
mutual ecstasy
and, maybe after some time, true love
that makes us both stronger
and happier
and that lasts forever
beyond our own lifespans.

OMAR RODRÍGUEZ

10 PRISONER WITHOUT A PRISON

*In Search of a Home
of Invisible Walls*

I am looking
to build with you a home
a space of transparent doors.

Glass ropes
silver floor
and invisible walls
where we could both
walk without restrictions.

So that being free, we wish to stay
and being imprisoned
we freely kiss
the metaphysical chain that binds us.

OMAR RODRÍGUEZ

11 THE TALISMAN

A Rare Find in the Freezing Waters

Today
  at the edge of a cold river
  I found a polished
and coral-like talisman
to take with me.

I found it in the freezing waters
mixed with sharp stones
and prismatic pebbles which in the past
have hurt my feet and wounded my touch.

Stubbornly, I kept my hand
in the river bed catching
this talisman
and I made it mine.

A unique one this talisman was, of rough appearance
which randomly touched my hand
as it was wandering lonely in the waters.

It knew how to touch, incisively
the intimate fibers
of the metaphysical essence of my soul
with inexplicable warmth
and solid, masculine
and translucent appearance.

Slowly
step by step
minute by minute
it melted
the frosty layers
covering my fingers' wounds
making them feel once again.

I will keep this prismatic talisman

very close to my heart and to my soul.

I will take care of it, polish it
and I will tell it my struggles and my failures
as well as the ups and downs of my life.

And God willing, one day it will fuse with the
skin of my chest
so that from then on
it accompanies me always
in my life's journey.

And this talisman, can you guess?
is you.

OMAR RODRÍGUEZ

12 METAPHYSICAL DISCOVERY

Simplifying the Form

I do not like wordy writings
because they say too little
in too many words.

I do not like wordy writings
because they sound simple without being so
and they take too long to reach the point.

What I have discovered today, my dear friend
I will say without superfluous words:
I love you.

Just that.
I love you.

Without preamble
or prologue
or anything else
and without elaborate words.

Simply...I love you.
Irremediably... I love you.
Without knowing how... I love you.
With no reason or sense of time... I love you.
Only that, dear friend. I love you.

And even if I try to escape
anticipating that I will end up hurting
without knowing how
I end up just at the same starting point:
I love you
just that, dear friend.
I love you.

13 I AND YOU

Confirming the Metaphysical
Distances with the Vernier

I and you.
You and I.

Perfect monosyllables
lonely one-sound words
that having been born alone
quickly learn to live together
and when they detach from each other
sting the eye and lacerate the soul.

You and I.
I and you.

Cosmic duality
which is fantastic and chimerical
living in two planes of different reality.

I, the passion - you, the embrace
You, the month - I, the day.

You watch me. I see you.
You hear me. I listen to you.
You like me. I love you.
You wanting friendship, I, desire.

Strange confusion of similar verbs
of parallel intensity
but painfully different.

You and I.
I and you.

Unbalanced reciprocity
where we think about each other
in unequal periods.
You of me, once a month
I of you, at every instant.

I at the Equator and you at the Pole
I, the elemental fire
You, the cold and mechanic battery flash
light.

You and I.
I and you.

Unknown to each other.
So close and yet so far
that the thread in the metaphysical needle
which knits us
seems to place us far apart from each other
in clothes worn by different people
in celestial bodies of diffuse and unequal intensity
and in colors of opposite brightness.

You and I.
I and you.

Fantastic duality
-- which could have been electric
intense
elemental
rustic and wild --
transforming itself today
into a hard and indifferent
lukewarm fantasy.

14 CLINGING TO YOU

Confirming the
Impossibility of Letting Go

C linging to the memory of you.

Of your strong voice
of your sweet laughter
of your light step
and of your torso.

Clinging to the idea of you.
To the warm memory of the time
when my mind imagined impatiently a fantasy
of mutual exchanges
that would never happen to me.

Clinging to you.
Tied up

molecularly holding on, stubbornly, to your
image
but never fully fused with you, like
oil and water
which being together never actually touch.

Clinging to you.
Impatiently waiting for a phone
that never rings
and a clock with a broken hand
that will never show
the time of our encounter.

Clinging to you.
Desperately.
Knowing, my love, that your thoughts
will fly away from me every day, every hour
like the parallel lines
which being aware of each other, never talk
and just watch each other from afar.

Clinging to you.
Lifeless, exhausted, almost defeated
with a broken back
a lowered guard
and a stunned face.

Clinging to you.
Without an exit, or luggage, or destination.
With the anxious hopelessness of the missed
train
in a freezing station full of people and noise
but empty of souls.

Clinging to you.
With the intimate certainty
that my memory will keep you
even when my brain wants to hide your
image
in the smallest and farthest neurons.

And even when my brain resists

and my tired memory chooses to forget you
a shiny and prismatic trace of you
will remain in my soul
to remind me of the days that I was
happily, and then desperately
intimately
secretly
and consistently
clinging
clinging to you.

15 KEY-LOSING FRIEND

The Opening of the Chamber

I mages.
Iridescent but somehow cloudy images
warm but stinging
like raindrops touching my skin at 100 km
per hour.

Images of a key-losing friend
who carelessly and naively
opened the moldy lock
of my warm chamber
and then, negligently, escaped
leaving the door wide open.

He escaped
the same way that fog unavoidably does
mischievously

through the mesh of our clothes.

He escaped
taking with him the magical key he used to
enter my chamber
perhaps losing it, my key-losing friend.

When he entered, he lit my warm, yet dark
chamber
with his ethereal luminosity
and his agile torso
and his masculine voice.

When he moved away, he left behind him an
ethereal trail.

I was so overwhelmed
and so stubbornly confused
that I could not close my door behind him.

I stayed there

open jawed

surprised

stunned

confused

but warm

enjoying the lukewarm feel of his magical trail

which felt less and less

while I needed it more and more.

When I tried to lock the door back
I couldn't.

The strong and heavy oak door
-- which had protected me in my latent state--
was swollen
stuck
and the grain of its wood was spilling golden honey
that tasted sour as rotten milk.

So, I stayed there

dear key-losing friend
with an expectant soul
emotionally touched
turned upside down
in my opened chamber.

And I often wonder
what I would do tomorrow
if you were to give me back the peace and
safety of a closed lock?

Or if the light from the window were to show
me
where you lost the key to my chamber?

Or if a kindhearted carpenter
were to offer to polish the hinges of my door
so that I could close it, and then return to my
latent
and defenseless – but comfortable-- state?

Undoubtedly, my key-losing friend
I would pretend not to see
and not to hear
concealing the furtive, indecent and illusion-
ary hope
that in the future
you might pass by again, naive and playful
carelessly and negligent
and make my senses feel again
with that fresh, ethereal and magical trail
that you took away with you
naively
when you left.

OMAR RODRÍGUEZ

16 THE MEMORIES WEAVER

Filling Your Absence

I am going to fill your absence
with the memories
that we both weaved in the dark.

Memories of a silent peace
built patiently
when I watched in awe
the bright golden particles
that lit kaleidoscopically
the pupil of your eyes
framing the dancing folds
of your playful and mischievous smile.

Memories of the burning drop

of a wax candle

lighting the profile of your naked torso.

And of your furtive whisper

stopped by my kiss, moist and warm

that trapped us for a few hours

in that world of ours

tiny and volatile

but with colorful wings of gigantic reach.

I am going to fill this, my absence of you

with the memories

that I patiently stored

in the silos of my senses.

I will feed myself

with the memories

that you left me with when you parted

until that unlikely day
when you may come back
to me.

OMAR RODRÍGUEZ

17 THE ALCHEMIST'S IMPRISONMENT

*Physiological Description of
a Metaphysical Phenomenon*

I t happened suddenly.

It must have happened in a careless moment:
-- during the brief instant of a respite
-- in the nanosecond of a quick blink
-- between two heart beats
-- or maybe at night, when dozing.

My soul
which had been protected for so long
well cared for
closed to emotions
and somehow stuck
untied to anything

got imprisoned, locked down, enclosed
suddenly, without knowing how
by the silver threads of your fantastical
form.

It was…inexplicable.

At first it was a whisper
then a voice
then a howl ripping the skin of my chest
clamoring to come out through my throat
while ten thousand butterflies were press-
ing, mischievously the thoracic cavity.

Breathlessness
persistent warmth in the cheeks
and an immense, desperate need for the
chest to burst
as the corn or the wheat in spring
or as the roots of trees when they break the
cement of the sidewalk

looking resolutely to expand.

It was such a new emotion
so different and overwhelming
but at the same time so warm
that my body overheated
and was inundated
with a comforting sense of completeness.

It was like a potent lightning bolt
that suddenly warmed up my whole being.

But it also brought:
-- the wet thunderstorm
-- the stinging of rapid rain on naked skin
-- the cold, uncomfortable sensation of wet
clothes over my warm body.

The rain on my window
perched itself on the glass
with its tiny drops, which being translucent

looked like small colored diamonds.

The warm fog of my irregular breathing
anxious and expectant
fogged up the glass of my window
at first warmly, then freezing
forming a sticky scab on the glass
making it hard to see your radiant light
which was slowly moving away
while my desperate eyes could not stop it
leaving behind a chained
contrite, expectant and hopeful soul.

I felt newly empty
with the same emptiness of the hands that
once held rain
and whose contents escaped, unstoppably
between the atoms of their fingers.

It happened suddenly.
And the strange metaphysical event left suddenly too
leaving behind a branding mark

that still burns now

as well as a soul in its prison of silk

perversely stuck in between the playfully knitted molecules

of your silver threads.

OMAR RODRÍGUEZ

18 THE ULTIMATUM

The Encounter of Two Ships

I know that by the end of this journey
I will be left without you
because I know that you will not love so strongly
as to fight
against the turbulent winds of your own tide.

Because I feel that when my ship passes near yours
you will ignore it
sailing on your set route
without adjusting your sails
to follow the uncertain route of my ship.

Because I fear that you will not have the courage
to follow me

taking you to different and wilder waters
-- I am not sure if better or safer—
but clearly far more distant
than you are accustomed to sail.

I will have to keep sailing
alone
the same way that I started
this journey.

My sails slack in the wind
free hand at the helm
sailing alone, with an open heart
the sails white
always facing forward
looking for a wind
to take me to a safe harbor
where I can anchor my ship.

Where I can share my life and my destiny
and my time

and the slow and heavy rhythm of my voice.

If you are not willing to change winds and seas
I won't alter the route of my ship
or stop
even to look at you.

Let's navigate together, if you want to
but with our faces high up towards the sun
our chests suntanned
and our skin aged by the elements and the sea salt.

Resisting together the wild winds
and risking together our lives
in each lightning and in each sea wave.

But don't ask me
to lower the mast of my sails
to the passing of other ships.

If I were to do that
I would be too weakened to raise it again
later
and we both would end up together, yes, but
looking at the ground
and more distant than ever.

Hold the sails of my ship
strongly against your naked chest as I pass
near you
or let them keep flapping in the air.

And if you choose to let them pass
-- as I painfully suspect that you will –
always remember
the white sails of this minuscule
and wild vessel
which one day crossed your way.

19 THE ABORTION

*Hunting, Extracting
and Letting Go of This
Loving Feeling*

I t hurts
like a profound incision
that stings the soul deeply.

It burns
searing each nervous fiber
each joint
flaying me alive.

It scorches
pitiless, leaving
the lashes tired
and the nose irritated.

It explodes

like an effervescent tablet in water
looking desperately for the exit.

I will look for it
rummaging, scratching, excavating until I
find it.

I will use lanterns
pikes
shovels
Geiger counters
until it can no longer hide its shiny halo
and I can catch it in a remote corner of my
soul
where it hides cautious and frightened.

I will use anesthesia and a sharp scalpel
salts and ethyl alcohol bought at the phar-
macy
to extract it
from the remote chamber where it lives.

I will set a net of miniscule mesh
just in case it is ephemeral and it tries to
vanish.

If necessary, I will offer a reward
and once it is captured in that net
I will look for a cosmic space to relocate it.

I will have it light a chandelier, a candle
some Christmas lights
or the golden wings of the Angel of Inde-
pendence.

Let it stay there
where somebody else impressed by its
brightness
makes it his.

Where it shines without burning
where it warms up without hurting

where it grows and expands without burst-
ing my chest or my brains
where it no longer swells the eyelids
once the eyes dry up and the thorax is heart
empty.

I will kick it out, even if it pains my soul
from the warm enclosure where it nested
suddenly.

I will expel it in a respite
in a tear
maybe in a desperate howl!

And when it flies ethereal to the heavens
I will say goodbye with a passionate kiss.

And it will phosphoresce in the cosmos with
its colorful trail
that once lit up
the most intimate

sensitive
and secret fibers of my soul.

OMAR RODRÍGUEZ

20 I HANG MY HANDKERCHIEF TO DRY

Farewell by Evaporation and Condensation

I hang my handkerchief to dry
to evaporate the tears
which saturate
soaking it
the weave of its fabric.

May these crystalline drops
of capricious and metaphysically changing
shapes sublimate
because they helped me shed my feelings for
you.

May those tears ascend to the stratosphere
so that they don't end up being stepped on
or dumped in the garbage bin
or carried by the dirty street sewage.

And once they are freed up
and ascend as steam to the cosmos
may they come back
condensed by a cloud
as rain.

And may this rain permeate, playfully
the molecular mesh of the fabric of your
clothes
touching every inch of your skin, your face
and your body
and deliver my final kiss
without you ever suspecting
their true origin.

21 THE SHIPWRECK

Lost in Turbulent Waters

Rusty iron, my frozen heart.
Whirlwind of ideas, my confused mind.
Unraveled tow, the lifeless muscles of my body.

Empty pots, the lachrymal glands of my eyes
and the palm of my hands.
Rugged desert, my lips.
Repellent oil, my touch that rejects other bodies different than yours.

And infinite loneliness, the instep of my naked foot
when lost in the emptiness of the bed

can't find yours anymore.

This is how I was left after you left.
After the thunderstorm.

Wet
anchored in you
while you were fleeing, fearful to sink with
me
in these turbulent waters.

Shipwrecked alone
waiting in vain for your support and rescue
wanting desperately to reach the shore
watching you fleeing me
I, holding tightly to a log
you, swimming swiftly to the beach.

22 ASHES

The Strange Nature of Metaphysical Residue

Please, my friend
don't stir up the memories.

Let the ashes of our life together
rest behind like you left them.
Even if they look cold from afar
they are still warm
and sometimes, they burn.

So, if you still have a sigh when you think of me
don't stir up the ashes.

If you can't change, dear friend
don't alter the peace
that I built in silence

OMAR RODRÍGUEZ

biting my lips
and learn, like me, to forget.

23 METAPHYSICAL JIGSAW PUZZLE

Trying to Put Together the Lost Atoms

I came back to pick up the pieces of me
that I left behind in these walls.

These walls of frozen concrete
that warmed up once
with the breathing
coming out from your lungs and my lungs.

Which, under the intermittent light of a candle
in the miniscule limits
of a warm and tiny world
where only you and I existed
made us self-reliant, sufficient
strong, loving and mutually giving.

I came back to pick up these pieces of me
that I badly need to be whole again.

I have not been able to live without them
and I walk the streets
empty, incomplete, stuck
with overwhelmed looks and my eyes to the
ground.

I will try to reassemble the pieces of me that I
am missing.
I will look for a carpenter to glue them
or a welder to weld them.
But it is so difficult!
There are so many and they are so scattered!

They are all over the place.
I shed them slowly and unknowingly
and now I see that they are atomized
in each molecule of this room

and in each spasm of my nervous breathing.

I find particles in the pillows
and in the bathroom
in the chimney and in the chest of drawers
in the door knobs
and in the sheets
and in the phone apparatus of the land line.

And wherever I touch
I find you intertwined in all these things
that still feel your touch
and distill your masculine scent
and the sweet and almost imperceptible
taste of your mouth
and the volatile vibration of your voice.

I close my eyes
and I can still feel your presence
and hear our voices that still vibrate in the
confines of this room

and can be perceived surrounding me in the
air.

I came here to pick up the pieces of me that I
left behind
and I realize with surprise
that they are far more than I thought at first.

They are too atomized.
They have nested
in the molecular structure of all the things
that form this simple room.

They are impregnated, interwoven
and resist leaving this room
to come back to their place of origin.

What can I do if they resist coming back to
me?
What can I do if these minuscule parts
have already tasted the texture of your com-
pany?

What can I do if they have already changed
their molecular structure
and they no longer fit back in my jigsaw puzzle?

I leave this room
crestfallen and incomplete, as I entered
knowing now that I have to part without
them.

Something from you and me
is meant to stay in this room eternally
and we cannot put it back together ever.

Some parts of us are meant to stay behind
this door
while I walk away
lonely and incomplete.

OMAR RODRÍGUEZ

24 THAT'S IT!

*Signing Out to Cauterize
the Wound*

That's it!
Because tonight
under the light of my red lamp
I have decided to forget you
and to close the door to your memories
that my soul has stubbornly held onto.

That's it!

Let's forget the feel of your warm touch
the taste of your lips
the safety of your wise hands
and the places
where we discovered together
the wild compatibility of our bodies.

To all that, That's it!

Let's forget the mutual glances
of deep intimacy
and the passionate kiss
and the pleasurable moan
guiding the touch wisely to the correct spot.

And our cosmos where time was invisible
and space was defined as the very short distance between your breathing and mine
where I got lost in the infinite vagueness
of a respite and an "I love you".

To all that, That's it!

Let's forget your head resting on my chest
and the firm intertwining of our hands
and the mischievous touch

and the passionate moan we used to explore
our bodies
and all that which we invented together
in eternal instants
and very short hours
playing infinite and chimerical games
of wild beauty.

To all that: That's it!

That's it!
Because it's time to sign off, once everything
has been said.

That's it!
Because in this music sheet
there is no space left for more notes, or keys,
or anything else
and there are only blank spaces
to fill with extra-large silences
that exclude flats or trembling sharps.

That's it!
To recharge batteries
to sharpen the pencil
to sign off a short episode of my life
which was shorter in your book than in
mine.

To all that
That's it!
Even if the soul sobs.

That's it!
Even if every body particle resists.

That's it!
Even if my nose misses your scent.

That's it!

Let's leave behind

the indelible impression of your playful smile in my pores

and use the light of my red lamp to light up the final paragraph

of this decided, firm and painful

That's it!

OMAR RODRÍGUEZ

25 FREEING THE PRISONER

*Rethinking the
Metaphysical Sentence*

e will have to rethink this case
in light of new evidence

and reluctantly, free the prisoner
who wanted to remain here
under a prison sentence.

We cannot keep him here
if he has to fight against your instinct and
your memories of others
putting on the breaks at every moment
and facing ghosts from your past every day
that he cannot touch, fight or vanish.

If it cannot be him who is hanging
from your neck chain
because that space is occupied by someone
else
we must free him
even if he stubbornly refuses.

We will have to absolve him
from the long sentence he is begging us to
give him
even if this pardon seems
more pitiless and crueler.

We will have to strip him of
that prison uniform
even if by doing it
we are throwing him naked
to the abyss!

26 BEYOND YOU

*Exiting the Prison and
Confronting the Fog
of the Future*

s I cross the lintel out of this
tearful and restless prison for good
I breathe easy looking ahead.

I walk hopeful, expectant and with ease out
of this chamber
where I was trapped.

Looking back
at this jail of cold walls for the last time
I leave being certain that it won't be you
where I will find
the answer to my questions
or the motive for my poems
or the shelter for my love.

Confronting the fog of the future
I ask myself
What will there be for me beyond you?

Beyond the confusing whirlpool of emotions
that you triggered in the sleeping fibers of
my body
beyond the unanswered sacrifice
and the waiting without response.

Beyond your playful and seductive smile
which never had the molecular structure to
fit my soul.

Beyond the world that surrounds you
and that you love
and which is hostile to me
and that made me understand
that I will never be your priority.

Beyond your words
that will never synch with mine
because their atomic composition
does not have the same number of particles
-- no less, no more –
only a different number
that I won't ever be able to change.

What will there be for me beyond you?

Beyond your habits
your delicious lips
the accelerated pulse of your veins
your masculine body
the warmth of your hands
and your extraordinary touch?

Reason.

The hope of finding someone
that does vibrate to my beat.

The exciting adventure
to find one day
another piece of my metaphysical jigsaw
puzzle
that better fits with my edges and contours
and who is able to receive that about me
that you will never be able to appreciate.

So, what will be there for me beyond you?
Freedom.
Redemption.

And with any luck, the true half
that I never found
in you.

27 THE CLOSED STORE

*Insufficient Funds
at the Counter*

I looked at my hand
and counted my coins.

The store clerk, indifferent
denied me entrance
for lack of funds in the correct currency.

I felt the horrible frustration
of looking at love, what I needed most
and being unable to get it.

I was just a few inches away from it
separated
by the armored counter

of transparent glass.

On the counter
the shiny inaccessible cash register was
theft-protected.

Anxiously I took a last peek
at the vast counter
until the clerks lowered the metal curtain
put on their jackets
and left to go home.

Meanwhile
the street fog spread on the sidewalk
while it became cold, lonely and late.

28 WHAT DOES IT MATTER!

Lost in the Monosyllables

What does it matter, my love
what I was for you
if I no longer am.
What does it matter!

What does it matter
what could have been
but wasn't.
If today it is not.
What does it matter!

What does it matter
if in your moments of leisure
you wanted to be
close to me
if today I don't know

a thing about you.
What does it matter!

What does it matter
if yesterday
you did want to see me
if today
when I am alone
I look for you and can't find you.
What does it matter!

If our bodies of yesterday
got fused very intimately
but today I'm alone
What does it matter, my love, what does it
matter!

If yesterday's hug
is no longer here
and your fleeting kiss is now gone
how does

that yesterday's memory
help me
reminding me of the place
where I am?

Since the past is now gone
And I can do nothing with it
What does it matter!

OMAR RODRÍGUEZ

29 FOURTEEN METAPHYSICAL REFLECTIONS

Synthesizing the Thoughts

I

In the absence of maps, fair rules
compasses and cartography charts
I must use the guide of my own instinct.

It shall never steer me wrong
it was given to me by God
to orient myself in the thunderstorm
and I shall never regret
the route that it tells me to follow.

II

I open to you now
in a simple and spontaneous verse
but you close up
in a long and profound silence

that solders your lock.

III

Y ou tell me
that you like me a lot.

Yet your absent touch and your distracted
mind
express a different reality
that I fail to understand.

IV

M y life goes by
like the cursed sower

seeding roses
and harvesting thorns.

V

I am the memory maker
picking up silver threads and knitting
stories.

And at the end of my journey
I only find dust, soot
an absent attic
and an empty pillow.

VI

My heart must be unusual.

When you approach the glass counter
you look at it, you try it, you say you like it
but you don't take it with you.

VII

I wish you were free, like me
to face your destiny with valor
instead of fleeing from yourself
against you own instincts.

VIII

How horrible
unwanted freedom is!

Blessed is the prisoner
who has given away his to a warden
that feeds him lovingly
every day.

IX

My memories of loves gone by
feel like the undertow

which comes back once in a while
weaker and less strong
but still wets my hand
and touches my clothes
and distends my heart
and stings my soul.

X

Double is the loneliness
of he who has had companionship.

Slower is the step
of he who has been agile.

Darker is the outlook
of he who has seen the light.

XI

If you don't come back to me my love
I want you, nevertheless, to be happy.
You deserve it.
Neither of us is at fault. Not you, not me.

Destiny has played against us.
The Spanish cards
have dealt us spades, instead of golden coins.

XII

Today I have figured out
that I should leave your life.

It is more painful to stay
than to bite my lip
and walk away.

Exhausted, almost dried up
with my batteries low
I must pack my things
close my heart
look away and flee from you.

XIII

Here, I am.
There, you are.

In between us
our uncertain future
which God willing
we shall explore
hand in hand together.

XIV

Every day, without missing one
I have been fed by your memories.

Every day, without missing one
your absence has pained me.

Every day, without missing one
I have told myself that you will never come
back.

But every day, without missing one
a spark of unlikely hope
keeps me alert and going.

EPILOGUE: CONVERSATIONS WITH MY PAST SELF

The Time Machine Dilemma

Reading the poems written by my past self

full of loneliness and self-searching
pain and longing
I had the impulse to create a time machine
so that I could visit him, talk to him and
cheer him up a little.

Hardware made of silver
cables of silk
powerful jet propulsion engine
modern on-line computer and remote control

powered with AAA batteries.

Dangerous trip this could have been
violating natural laws
and time directives
full of threatening time paradoxes
as revelations about the future to my past
self
could surely alter my life in the present.

So I gave up.

I couldn't risk my present
on such time travel adventure.

Most of all, I couldn't risk losing
the companion I found
in this vibrant place that became my adopted
home
where we have lived together for so long.

Where we have shared everything
the same house
the same dishes
the same alarm clock
and the same pillow.

Where we share our problems and hopes
and at the end of each day
I am kissed on the forehead
before I go to bed.

Where there is no "you" or "me"
but "us".
Our life
our home
our longings
our hopes and our wishes.

Where every day we wash our backs
and brush our teeth

and carry out our daily work
and at the end of each day
we long to be with each other to feel safe and
complete
watching TV together, reading a book, playing a game
or dancing a two-step feeling each other's
heart beating next to our own.

Where every day we grow old together.

Oh, yes
definitely
I will abandon my time machine
and burn its blueprints at once!

I should let my past self build his own future
by himself
and prevent my future self from being

tempted
to interfere with mine one day.

I shall live in the present, and so should my
past self too
without knowing the future in advance!

OMAR RODRÍGUEZ

THE AUTHOR

Omar Rodríguez is an actor (aka Omar Chagall) who wrote his first poem in México at age 8 after reading the poetry of Sor Juana Inés de la Cruz and Jose Martí.

His style is inspired mostly by León Felipe and Federico García Lorca. His favorite painter is Remedios Varo, whose magical surrealism is a source of inspiration about the mystical and the metaphysical.

He acted in *The Sopranos*, *Law & Order*, *Unforgettable* and other TV series. In film he was in *Frida*, *Romero*, and in *Che Part 1*. He has also appeared in theater in a variety of plays, including off Broadway. Omar is a proud union member of SAG/AFTRA and AEA.

In 2016 he retired from a parallel business consulting career with an international firm.

Omar is also an international and national award-winning stamp collector who specializes in the early stamps of México.

He has an MBA (University of Wisconsin-Madison), an MFA (New School-Actor's Studio in NYC) and a BA (EBC México). Born in México City he moved to New York a long time ago where he lives happily with his husband Glen, the love of his life.

He welcomes any reactions to his poetry through OmarPoesia@aol.com

Made in the USA
Middletown, DE
15 June 2021